INSECTS UP CLOSE

Grasshoppers

by Patrick Perish

BLASTOFF! READERS

BELLWETHER MEDIA · MINNEAPOLIS, MN

Note to Librarians, Teachers, and Parents:

Blastoff! Readers are carefully developed by literacy experts and combine standards-based content with developmentally appropriate text.

Level 1 provides the most support through repetition of high-frequency words, light text, predictable sentence patterns, and strong visual support.

Level 2 offers early readers a bit more challenge through varied simple sentences, increased text load, and less repetition of high-frequency words.

Level 3 advances early-fluent readers toward fluency through increased text and concept load, less reliance on visuals, longer sentences, and more literary language.

Level 4 builds reading stamina by providing more text per page, increased use of punctuation, greater variation in sentence patterns, and increasingly challenging vocabulary.

Level 5 encourages children to move from "learning to read" to "reading to learn" by providing even more text, varied writing styles, and less familiar topics.

Whichever book is right for your reader, Blastoff! Readers are the perfect books to build confidence and encourage a love of reading that will last a lifetime!

This edition first published in 2018 by Bellwether Media, Inc.

No part of this publication may be reproduced in whole or in part without written permission of the publisher. For information regarding permission, write to Bellwether Media, Inc., Attention: Permissions Department, 5357 Penn Avenue South, Minneapolis, MN 55419.

Library of Congress Cataloging-in-Publication Data

Names: Perish, Patrick.
Title: Grasshoppers / by Patrick Perish.
Description: Minneapolis, MN : Bellwether Media, Inc., 2018. | Series:
    Blastoff! Readers. Insects Up Close | Audience: Age 5-8. | Audience: K to
    grade 3. | Includes bibliographical references and index.
Identifiers: LCCN 2016057235 (print) | LCCN 2017007900 (ebook) | ISBN
    9781626176652 (hardcover : alk. paper) | ISBN 9781681033952 (ebook)
Subjects: LCSH: Grasshoppers–Juvenile literature.
Classification: LCC QL508.A2 P47 2018 (print) | LCC QL508.A2 (ebook) | DDC
    595.7/26–dc23
LC record available at https://lccn.loc.gov/2016057235

Editor: Christina Leighton   Designer: Maggie Rosier

Printed in the United States of America, North Mankato, MN.

Table of Contents

What Are Grasshoppers?

Grasshoppers have powerful legs. These insects are super jumpers!

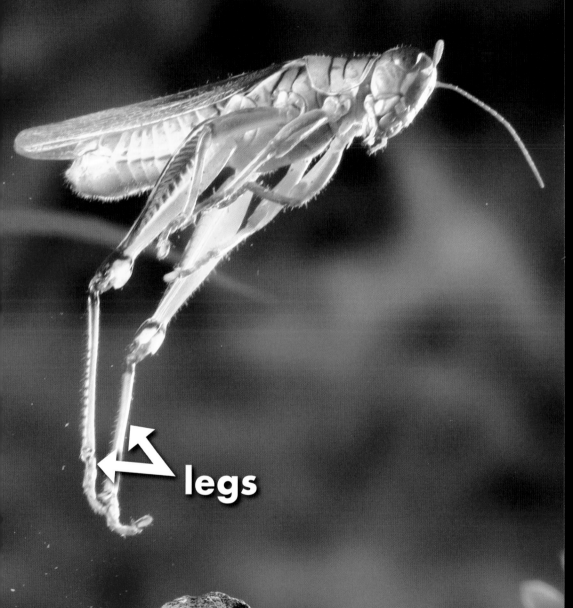

legs

Grasshoppers have short **antennae**. They use these to smell and feel.

antennae

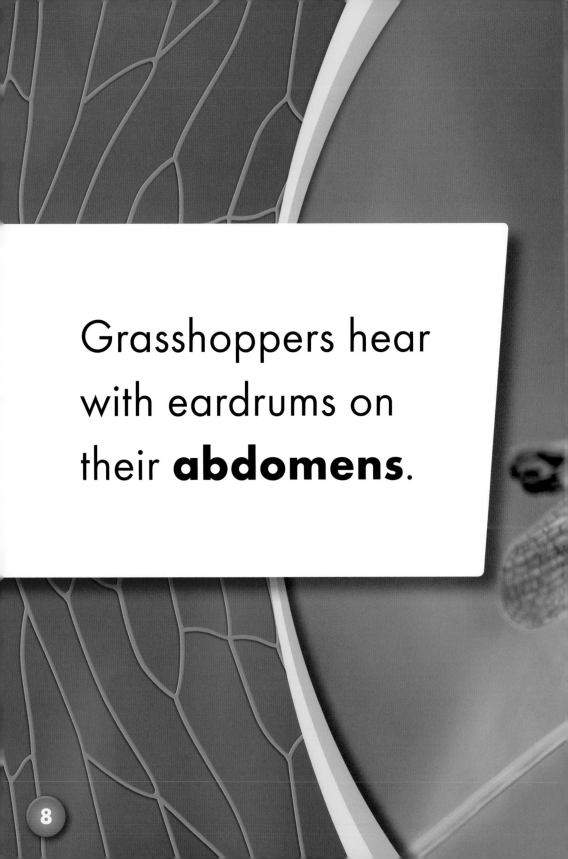

Grasshoppers hear with eardrums on their **abdomens**.

eardrum

abdomen

ACTUAL SIZE:
Carolina grasshopper

Hoppers at Home

Many grasshoppers make homes in forests and fields. They are busy during the day.

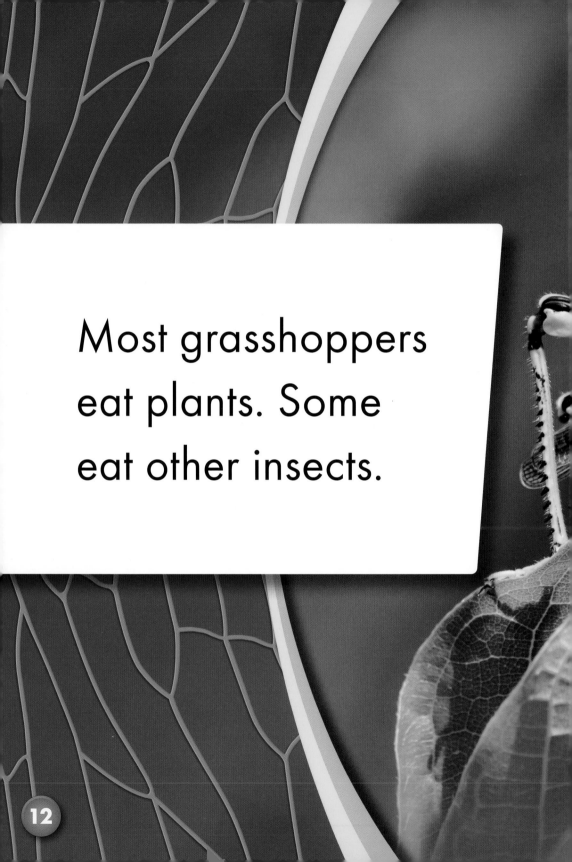

Most grasshoppers eat plants. Some eat other insects.

FAVORITE FOOD:

alfalfa

Grasshoppers rub their legs against their wings to make sounds. This is how they talk.

wing

legs

Thousands of grasshoppers may **swarm**. They eat **crops** and bother farmers.

Growing Up

Female grasshoppers lay eggs in summer. **Nymphs** break out of eggs in spring.

female
grasshopper

nymphs

eggs

19

Nymphs **molt** to become adults. Soon, they can fly and jump high!

molting

GRASSHOPPER
LIFE SPAN:
about 1 year

Glossary

abdomens

the back parts of insect bodies

molt

to shed skin for growth

antennae

feelers connected to the head that sense information around them

nymphs

young insects; nymphs look like small adults without full wings.

crops

plants grown by farmers

swarm

to gather in one place; thousands of insects swarm together.

To Learn More

AT THE LIBRARY

Bodden, Valerie. *Grasshoppers.* Mankato, Minn.: Creative Education, 2014.

Lunis, Natalie. *Giant Weta: The World's Biggest Grasshopper.* New York, N.Y.: Bearport Publishing, 2013.

Schuh, Mari. *Grasshoppers.* Minneapolis, Minn.: Jump!, 2015.

ON THE WEB

Learning more about grasshoppers is as easy as 1, 2, 3.

1. Go to www.factsurfer.com.

2. Enter "grasshoppers" into the search box.

3. Click the "Surf" button and you will see a list of related web sites.

With factsurfer.com, finding more information is just a click away.

Index

The images in this book are reproduced through the courtesy of: Kirsanov Valeriy Vladimirovich, front cover; Michael Durham/ Minden Pictures/ SuperStock, pp. 4-5; Glass and Nature, pp. 6-7; Rudmer Zwerver, pp. 8-9; Patricia Hofmeester, pp. 10-11; Leena Robinson, pp. 12-13; Boonchuay1970, p. 13; Tyler Fox, pp. 14-15; Ingo Arndt/ Minden Pictures, pp. 16-17, 22 (bottom right); Mitsuhiko Imamori/ Minden Pictures/ SuperStock, pp. 18-19; kurt_G, pp. 19, 22 (center right); Cathy Keifer, pp. 20-21, 22 (top right); Jan-Nor Photography, p. 22 (top left); Hajakely, p. 22 (center left); Aleksandar Milutinovic, p. 22 (bottom left).